Selsam, Millicent Ellis
A first look at seashells.

A FIRST LOOK AT SEASHELLS

By Millicent E. Selsam
and Joyce Hunt

ILLUSTRATED BY HARRIETT SPRINGER

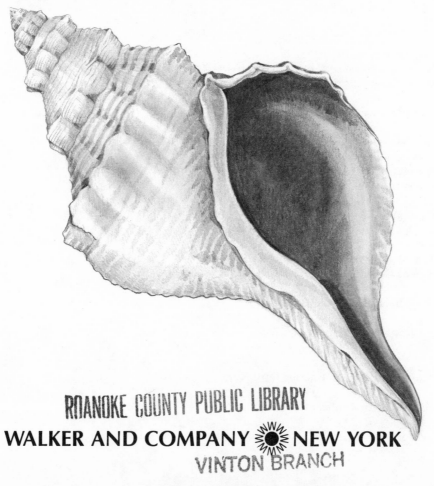

WALKER AND COMPANY ✹ NEW YORK

Library of Congress Cataloging in Publication Data

Selsam, Millicent Ellis, 1912—
    A first look at seashells.

    (A first look at series)
    Summary: An introduction to seashells, explaining how
they are classified and describing the differences that
distinguish one kind of seashell from another.
    1. Shells—Juvenile literature. [1. Shells.
2. Mollusks. 3. Seashore biology] I. Hunt, Joyce.
II. Springer, Harriett, ill. III. Title. IV. Series:
Selsam, Millicent Ellis, 1912–   . First look at series.
QL405.2.S44 1983   594′.0471   83-5876
ISBN 0-8027-6502-5
ISBN 0-8027-6503-3 (lib. bdg.)

First published in the United States of America
in 1983 by the Walker Publishing Company, Inc.

Published simultaneously in Canada by John Wiley
& Sons Canada, Limited, Rexdale, Ontario.

This edition printed in 1985.

ISBN: 0-8027-6503-3 Reinforced

Library of Congress Catalog Card Number: 83-5876

Printed in the United States of America

10   9   8   7   6   5   4   3

A *FIRST LOOK AT* SERIES

A FIRST LOOK AT LEAVES
A FIRST LOOK AT FISH
A FIRST LOOK AT MAMMALS
A FIRST LOOK AT BIRDS
A FIRST LOOK AT INSECTS
A FIRST LOOK AT FROGS AND TOADS
A FIRST LOOK AT SNAKES, LIZARDS, AND OTHER REPTILES
A FIRST LOOK AT ANIMALS WITH BACKBONES
A FIRST LOOK AT ANIMALS WITHOUT BACKBONES
A FIRST LOOK AT FLOWERS
A FIRST LOOK AT THE WORLD OF PLANTS
A FIRST LOOK AT MONKEYS AND APES
A FIRST LOOK AT SHARKS
A FIRST LOOK AT WHALES
A FIRST LOOK AT CATS
A FIRST LOOK AT DOGS
A FIRST LOOK AT HORSES
A FIRST LOOK AT DINOSAURS
A FIRST LOOK AT SPIDERS
A FIRST LOOK AT SEASHELLS

Each of the nature books in this series is planned to develop the child's powers of observation—to train him or her to notice distinguishing characteristics. A leaf is a leaf. A bird is a bird. An insect is an insect. That is true. But what makes an oak leaf different from a maple leaf? Why is a hawk different from an eagle, or a beetle different from a bug?

Classification is a painstaking science. These books give a child the essence of the search for differences that is the basis for scientific classification.

For Katie

Thanks are due to Dr. William K. Emerson,
Curator, Department of Invertebrates,
American Museum of Natural History,
for checking the manuscript and illustrations
of this book.

Where the land meets the sea we find seashells.

There are many different kinds.
They can be round like the moon, long like a jackknife,
or shaped like boxes, fans or tops.

The shells we find are usually empty but once
there were soft bodies inside.
Animals with hard shells outside and soft bodies inside
are called *mollusks* (MOL-usks).

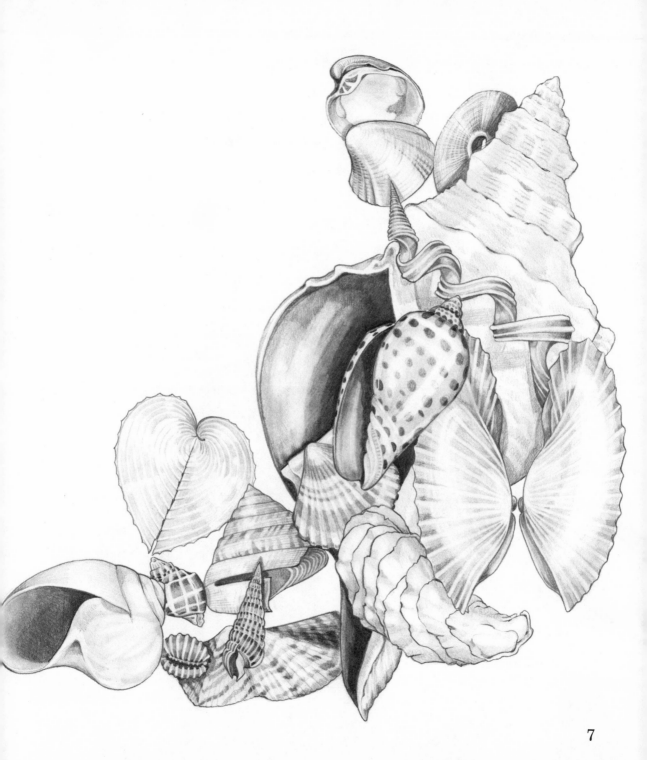

7

Most of the shells you find on the beach
can be put into two big groups.
One group has only one shell, like a snail.
We call this group *univalves* (*uni* means one).

MOON SNAIL

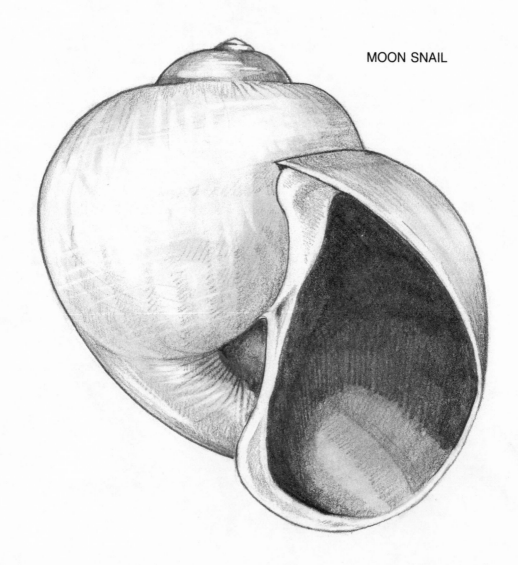

The other group has two shells, like a clam.
We call this group *bivalves* (*bi* means two).

QUAHOG

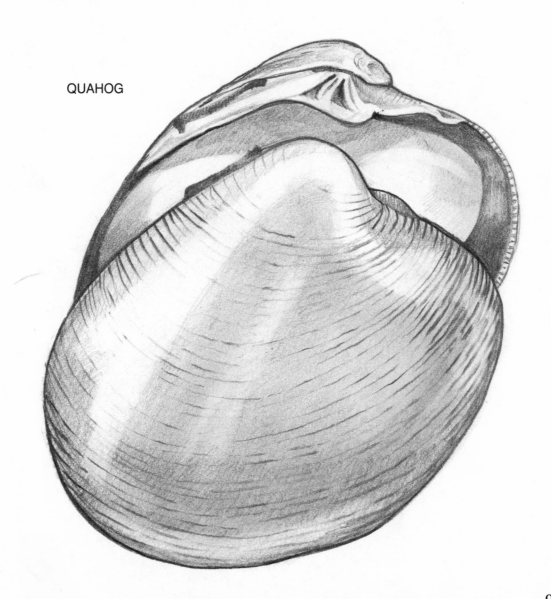

Which of these shells are univalves?
Which are bivalves?

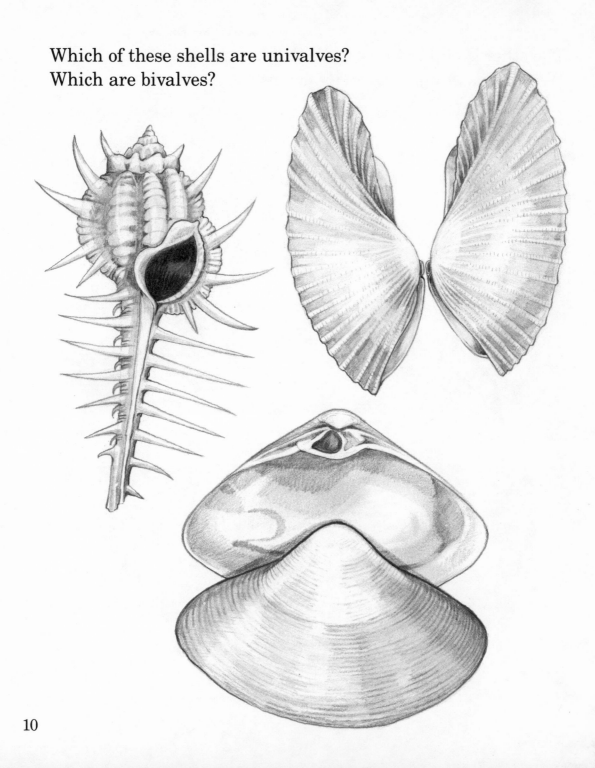

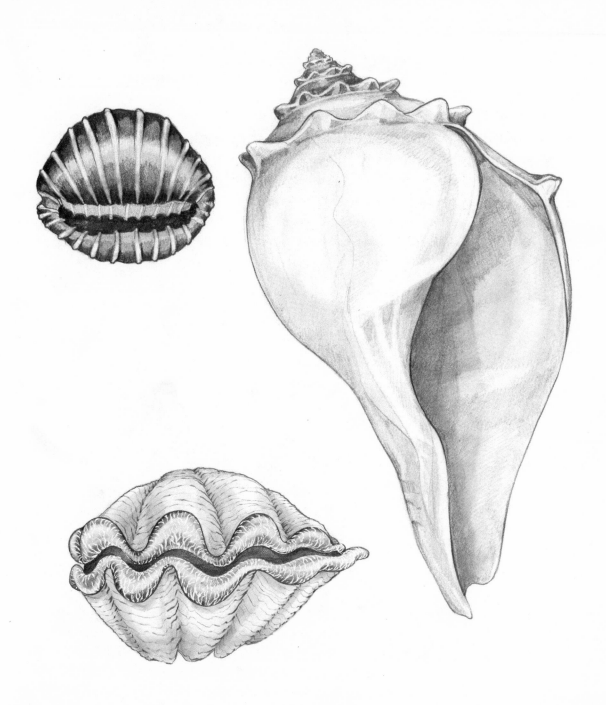

BIVALVES OR CLAMS

How do you tell bivalves apart?
Many bivalves are named for what they look like.
Match each bivalve to its name.

ANGEL WINGS
JACKKNIFE CLAM
SPINY OYSTER
KITTEN'S PAW
LONG-HANDLED DIPPER SHELL

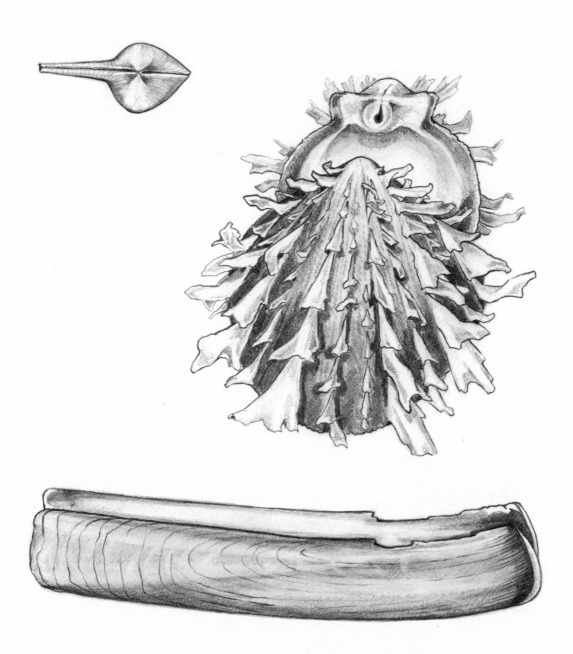

The *soft-shell clam* gets *its* name from its shell,
which is soft enough to crack with your fingers.

Most clams have hard shells.
You can tell these two hard-shelled clams apart
by looking at the *beak* and *hinge*.

The *Venus clam* or *quahog* (KO-hog) has three teeth
at the top of its hinge. The beak
is twisted to one side.
The *surf clam* has a little pocket
at the top of its hinge. The beak
is in the middle.
Which is which?

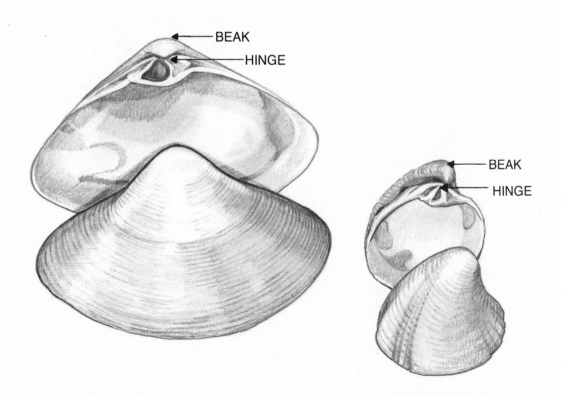

BEAK

HINGE

BEAK

HINGE

There are special ways to tell these bivalves apart.

Which shell is dark and has tiny threads
that anchor it to rocks?
(The threads are called its "beard.")

Which shell has tiny "wings" on each side of its beak?
(The "wings" are also called "ears.")

Which shell is thick, rough, and bumpy?
(It looks like a rock.)

Which shell has uneven valves?
The smaller valve has a hole near the top.
(It is sometimes called a *Mermaid's Toenail*.)

OYSTER

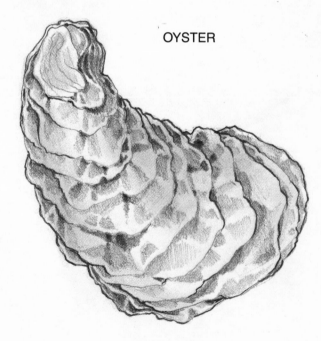

JINGLE SHELL

MUSSEL

SCALLOP

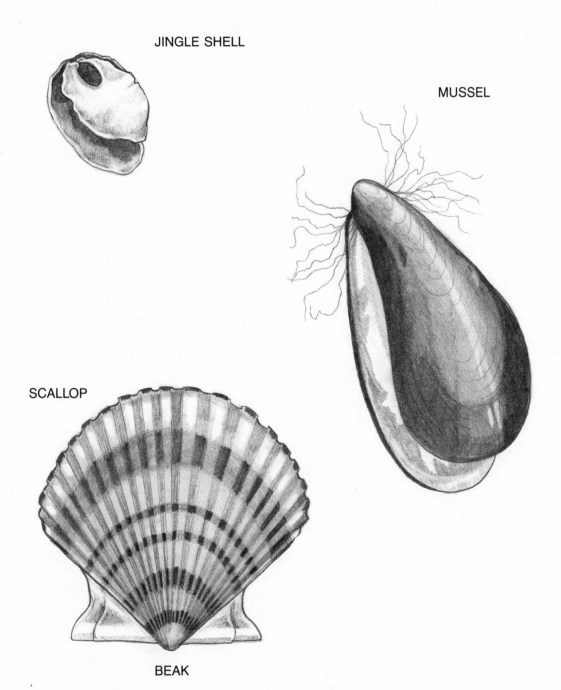

BEAK

17

The shape of these bivalves helps to tell them apart.
When the *cockle shell* is closed, it looks like a heart.

When the *ark shell* is closed it looks like a small pocketbook.
Notice the long, straight hinge with many teeth.

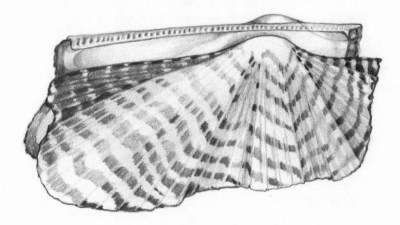

Sometimes size is a clue.
The *giant clam* is the largest bivalve.
It can get to be four feet long.

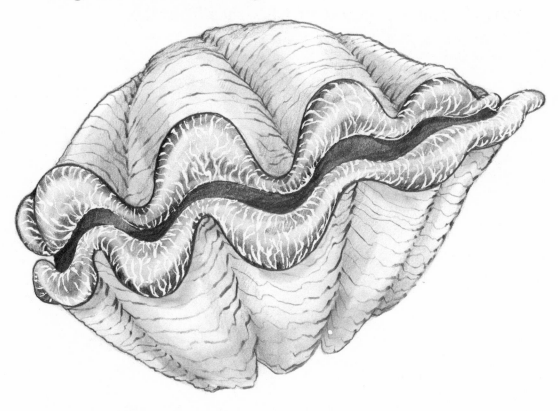

The *nut clam* is one of the smallest bivalves.
It only gets to be 1/3 of an inch long.

UNIVALVES OR SNAILS

How do you tell univalves apart?
Many of them are named for what they look like.
Match each univalve to its name.

HELMET SHELL
CONE SHELL
WORM SHELL
SLIPPER SHELL

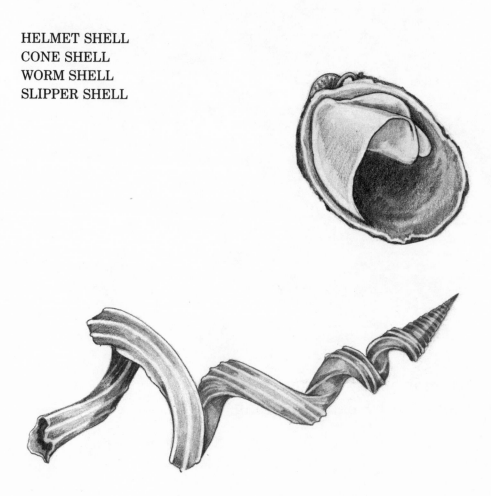

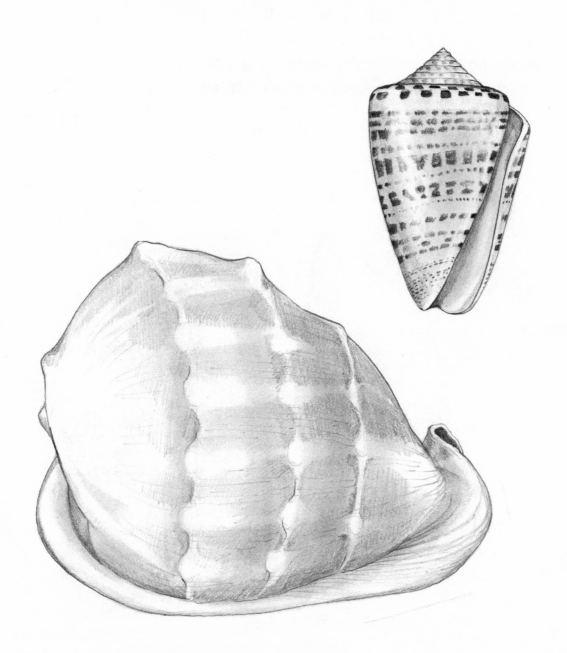

You can tell some univalves apart
by looking at the opening of the shell.
Which one has a smooth, round opening?
Which one has an opening edged with teeth?

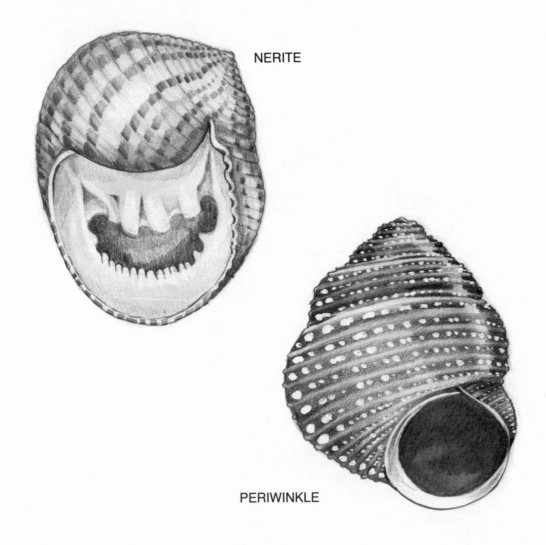

NERITE

PERIWINKLE

The *cowrie* also has teeth but the
opening is long and narrow like a partly
opened mouth.
The shell is smooth and shiny.

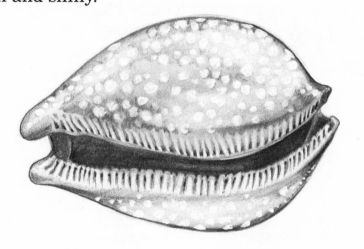

The *trivia shell* looks like a small, wrinkled cowrie.

Here are the kind of shells you hold to your ear
to hear sea sounds. (You are really hearing
air going through the shell.)

A *conch* and a *whelk* look alike.
But only the conch has a notch.

The *murex* looks like the whelk with spines.

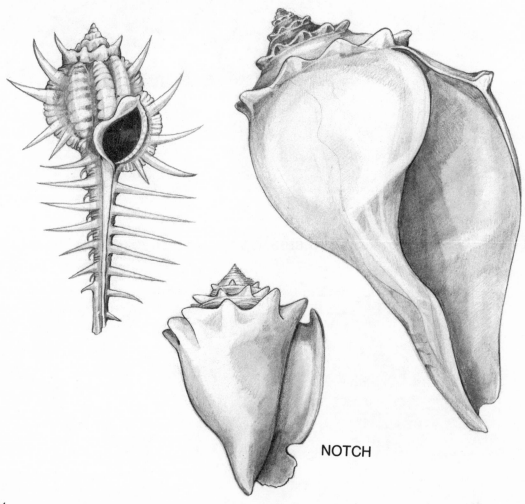

NOTCH

Sometimes univalves have small openings on the shell.
Find the *abalone* with small holes in a row.
Find the *limpet* with one hole in the middle of the shell.
This limpet is called a *keyhole limpet*. Do you see why?

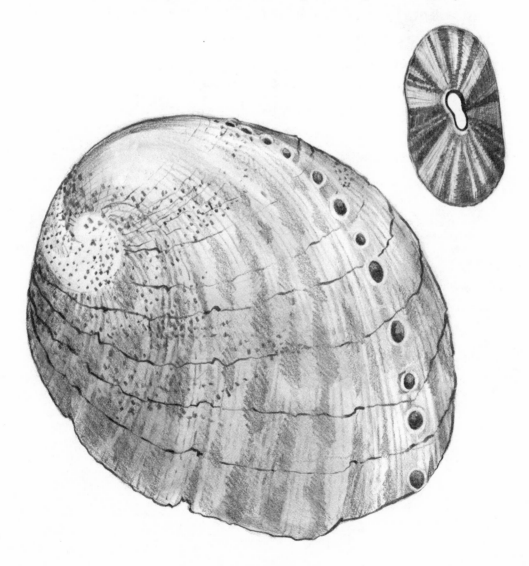

You can easily mix up these two shells.
One is called a *turban shell*.
The other is called a *top shell*.
But there is one sure way to tell them apart.
When an animal is inside the shell, it closes a little
trap door called an *operculum* (oh-PER-kew-lum)
that covers the opening.
The operculum of the top shell has lines.
The operculum of the turban shell has no lines.

Both of these shells look like screws.
But the operculum of the *turret shell* is round.
The operculum of the *auger shell* looks like a claw.
Which is which?

You can tell some univalves
by the pattern on the shell.

Find the one with round spots.
Find the one with square spots.
Find the one with many thin stripes.
Find the one with four wide stripes.

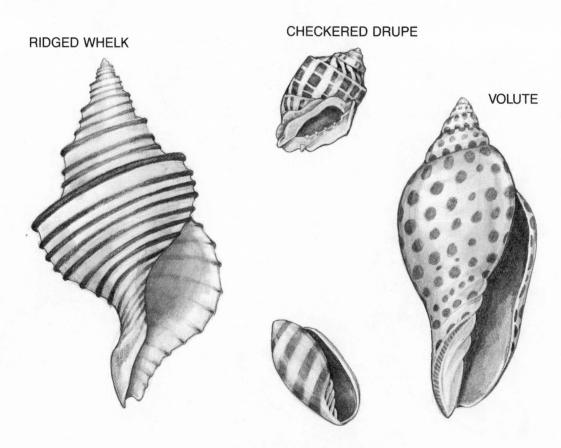

RIDGED WHELK

CHECKERED DRUPE

VOLUTE

ORANGE-BANDED MARGINELLA

Sometimes size is a clue.
The *horse conch* is one of the largest univalves.

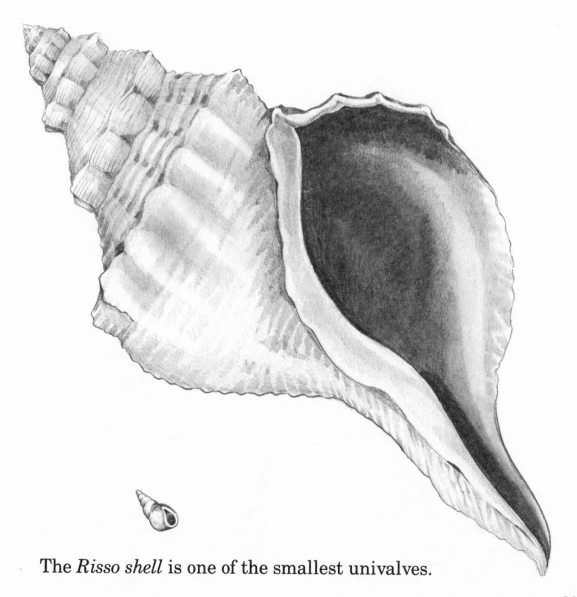

The *Risso shell* is one of the smallest univalves.

To tell bivalves apart:

Look at the shape.

Look at the size.

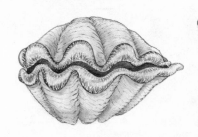

Look at the hinge and teeth.

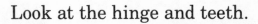

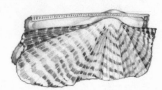

Look at the beak.

Look for uneven valves.

Look for "wings" and threads.

 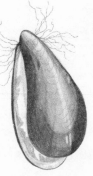

30

To tell univalves apart:

Look at the shape.

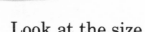

Look at the size.

Look at the opening.

Look at the operculum.

Look for notches and spines.

 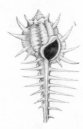

Look for holes.

Look for patterns.

SEASHELLS IN THIS BOOK